The Hummel
Friendship Book

with authentic Hummel pictures

ars edition

A faithful friend is a strong defense,
and he that finds such finds a treasure.
A faithful friend is beyond price,
and there is no weighing of his goodness.
A faithful friend is the medicine of life.

Ecclesiasticus

Wherever you are, it is your friends
who make your world.

Henry James

Our friends are chosen for us
by some hidden law of sympathy
and not by our conscious will.

Randolf Bourne

Old friends is always best,
'less you can catch a new one
that's fit to make an old one out of.

Sarah Orne Jewett

A friend is a person
with whom I may be sincere.
Before him, I may think aloud.

Ralph Waldo Emerson

True friendship
is a plant of slow growth,
and must undergo and withstand
the shocks of adversity
before it is entitled
to that appellation.

George Washington

The reward of friendship is itself.

St. Ailred de Rievaulx

Where your friends are,
There your riches are.

Latin proverb

True friendship is never severe.

Marie, Marquise de Sévigné

A friend is a poem.

Persian proverb

But true love is a durable fire,
In the mind ever burning,
Never sick, never old, never dead,
From itself never turning.

Sir Walter Raleigh

Give All to love;
Obey thy heart;
Friends, Kindred, days,
Estate, good-fame,
Plans, credit and the Muse –
Nothing refuse.

Ralph Waldo Emerson

Great beauty, great strength,
and great riches are really
and truly of no great use:
a right heart exceeds them all.

Benjamin Franklin

Himmel

A true friend
is the greatest of all blessings,
and the one which we take the least care
to acquire.

François de la Rochefoucauld

If a man should ascend alone
into heaven and behold clearly
the structure of the universe
and the beauty of the stars,
there would be no pleasure for him
in the awe-inspiring sight,
which would have filled him
with delight if he had someone
to whom he could describe
what he had seen.

Cicero

There is nothing we like to see
so much as the gleam of pleasure
in a person's eye when he feels
that we have sympathized with him,
understood him, interested ourself
in his welfare. At these moments,
something fine and spiritual
passes between two friends.
These moments are the moments
worth living.

Don Marquis

A true friend unbosoms freely,
advises justly, assists readily,
adventures boldly, takes all
patiently, defends courageously,
and continues a friend unchangeably.

William Penn

Friends will live not only
in harmony but in melody.

Henry David Thoreau

I am wealthy in my friends.

Shakespeare

Let not the grass grow
on the path of friendship.

American Indian saying

Friends share all things.

Pythagoras

The finest kind of friendship
is between people who expect
a great deal of each other
but never ask it.

Sylvia Bremer

Friendship is the source of the
greatest pleasures, and without
friends even the most agreeable
pursuits become tedious.

St. Thomas Aquinas

The only way to have a friend
is to be one.

Ralph Waldo Emerson

I shot an arrow in the air,
It fell to earth I knew not where;
For, so swiftly it flew, the sight
Could not follow it in its flight.

I breathed a sing into the air,
It fell to earth, I knew not where;
For who has sight so keen and strong,
That it can follow the flight of song?

Long, long afterward, in an oak
I found the arrow, still unbroke;
and the song from beginning to end,
I found again in the heart of a triend.

Henry Wadsworth Longfellow

The ornament of a house
is the friends who frequent it.

Ralph Waldo Emerson

Friendship makes prosperity
more brilliant, and lightens
adversity by dividing and
sharing it.

-        Cicero

What is a friend? A single
soul dwelling in two bodies.

Aristotle

Hold a true friend with both
your hands.

Nigerian proverb

A friend may well be reckoned
the masterpiece of nature.

Ralph Waldo Emerson

True friendship is like sound health;
the value of it is seldom known
until it be lost.

Charles Caleb Colton

Make all good men your well-wishers,
and then, in the years' steady sifting,
some of them turn into friends.
Friends are the sunshine of life.

John Hay

Lead me not, I will not follow;
Follow me not, I will not lead;
But walk with me, and be my friend.

Jack Gebel

Friends depart, and memory
takes them to her caverns,
pure and deep.

Thomas Haynes Bayly

My heart is warm with the friends I make,
And better friends I'll not be knowing.

Edna St. Vincent Millay

We at Ars Edition hope this little book has brought you pleasure. The pages of this collector's edition are folded back-to-back, in a style known as Japanese binding. You may wish to collect all these beautiful Hummel books:

The Hummel Friendship Book
The Hummel Thank You Book
The Hummel Get Well Book
The Hummel Birthday Book

For the store nearest you which carries our Hummel books, please write us.

ars edition inc.

"The Original Hummel People"

70 Air Park Drive, Ronkonkoma, NY 11779

© 1983 ars edition · all rights reserved
arranged and edited by Jonathan Roth
printed in West Germany · ISBN 0-86724-051-2